T5-DHA-657

Headings for Tomorrow

Public Access Display of Subject Headings

Prepared by the
Subcommittee on the Display
of Subject Headings
in Subject Indexes in Online
Public Access Catalogs,
Subject Analysis Committee,
Cataloging and Classification Section,
Association for Library Collections
and Technical Services

American Library Association
Chicago and London, 1992

Cover designed by Charles Bozett

Text designed by Dianne Rooney

Composed by Digital Graphics, Inc./Blue Pencil Creative Group, Ltd. in ITC Bookman using FrameMaker.

Printed on 50-pound Finch Opaque, a pH-neutral stock, and bound in 10-point CIS cover stock by IPC, St. Joseph, Michigan.

The paper used in this publication meets the minimum requirements of American National Standard for Information Sciences— Permanence of Paper for Printed Library Materials, ANSI Z39.48-1984. ⊗

Library of Congress Cataloging-in-Publication Data
Headings for tomorrow : public access display of subject headings / pre-
    pared by the Subcommittee on the Display of Subject Headings in
    Subject Indexes in Online Public Access Catalogs, Subject Analysis
    Committee, Cataloging and Classification Section, Association for
    Library Collections and Technical Services.
        p.   cm.
    Includes bibliographical references.
    ISBN 0-8389-3414-5 (alk. paper)
    1. Catalogs, On-line— Subject access— Standards— United States.
    2. Subject headings, Library of Congress— Evaluation.
    3. Information display systems— Library applications.
    4. Information display systems— Formatting.   5. Machine-readable
    bibliographic data.   6. Subject cataloging— Data processing.   7. On-
    line bibliographic searching.   I. American Library Association.
    Subcommittee on the Display of Subject Headings in Subject Indexes
    in Online Public Access Catalogs.
    Z699.35.S92H43   1992
    825.3'132— dc20   92-14484

Printed in the United States of America.

96 95 94 93 92   5 4 3 2 1

Contents

— ▬ ▬ ▬ ▬ ▬ ▬ —

Notes   50

Introduction

The following guide is intended to aid system designers and librarians involved in making decisions about the design of displays of more than one subject heading to users of online public access catalogs. The focus is on subject headings derived from the *Library of Congress Subject Headings (LCSH)*, although the principles explored would be applicable to similar lists of highly structured subject heading strings.

This guide was prepared by the Subcommittee on the Display of Subject Headings in Subject Indexes in Online Public Access Catalogs, of the Subject Analysis Committee, Cataloging and Classification Section, Association for Library Collections and Technical Services, American Library Association (ALA). In 1987, the subcommittee was formed and charged as follows: To study current online catalogs to determine problems with displays of subject headings in subject indexes; to recommend solutions to problems with displays of subject headings in subject indexes in online catalogs, in the form of published guidelines for distribution to system designers and librarians involved in decision-making about online catalogs.

Members of the subcommittee were Liz Bishoff, Karen M. Drabenstott, Joan S. Mitchell, Stephen Van Houten, and Martha M. Yee, Chair.

The term "guide" is being used so that it is clear that this publication is not meant to function as a standard that prescribes or even recommends certain decisions. It is meant, rather, as a map to a complex territory. The complexities may be unfamiliar even to those who have had experience with Library of Congress (LC) subject headings. The library world has never adopted a standard for the arrangement of headings, that is, a standard set of filing rules. Rather, several standards have existed and libraries have developed their own in-house practices to meet local needs. Accordingly, this guide makes recommendations only where there appears to be little question about the most desirable way to solve a problem. In other cases, it presents pro and con arguments on each issue. Thus, each online system may adopt its own solutions based on an informed analysis of the issues involved.

The committee was charged to limit the scope of the guide to questions about display and to exclude discussion of indexing and file structure, but this was sometimes difficult. For example, the question of whether to display the name of a person as author together with the name of the person as subject is clearly an indexing and file structure question as well as a display question.

The subcommittee began its work in 1987 with a survey of existing online systems. Because systems are under continuous development, data collected at that time may now be out of date, so we have not attempted to report on displays of individual systems. We make some generalizations based on this earlier research in our descriptions of "current practice," but we urge readers to use this information with care. Our observations of current practice do not imply any sort of standard or better way of doing things. We observed much in current practice in online systems that is probably *not* the best way of doing things; many practices probably resulted from lack of forethought, lack of resources, or the inability to solve intractable programming problems, rather than from a principled consideration of user needs.

The Structured Approach and the Strict Alphabetical Approach

Examination of existing sets of filing rules written after the advent of the computer reveals two different guiding philosophies. The "structured approach" is embodied in *The Li-*

brary of Congress Filing Rules (1980).[1] The "strict alphabetical approach" is partially embodied in *The ALA Filing Rules* (1980), although it, too, takes a structured approach to chronological subdivisions.[2] Most current online public access catalogs follow the alphabetical approach even more strictly than the ALA rules call for. In the more detailed discussions of arrangement issues that make up the guide, we found that the same pro and con arguments occurred repeatedly. We felt that it might be useful to summarize them in the introduction.

The "structured approach," put most simply, arranges headings based on the categories to which they belong. For example, history headings are arranged chronologically rather than alphabetically. To do this, the structured approach uses the concept of the filing element: headings are divided into more than one filing element and arrangement is based on the initial filing element alone. Only when two headings have the same initial filing element are they subarranged by the next filing element. These filing elements are identified, by means of subfield codes in the USMARC Format for Bibliographic Data (MARC) and/or by means of punctuation, as being certain types of data. Thus, chronological subdivisions have a different subfield code from geographical subdivisions. This coding allows computer programs to arrange them chronologically rather than alphabetically. Perhaps all of this may be more clearly seen in the examples below of Library of Congress subject headings arranged according to the structured approach:

Water—Abstracts.
Water—Aeration.
Water—Aeration—Congresses.
Water—Bibliography.
Water—Congresses.
Water—Dictionaries.
Water—Economic aspects.
Water—Handbooks, manuals, etc.
Water—Law and legislation—Italy.
Water—Pollution—Nevada.
Water—Study Guides.
Water—Translations from Russian.
Water—California—Congresses.
Water—Great Lakes Region.

Water— United States— Congresses.
Water beds (Furniture)
Water buffalo.
Water clocks.
Water conservation— Kansas.
Water districts.
Water ferns.
Water hammer.
Water in agriculture.
Water-meters.
Water pollution control industry.
Water quality— Pennsylvania— Philadelphia.
Water repellents.
Water resources development— California.
Water skiing.
Water softening sludge.
Water spirits in literature.
Water-supply— California.
Water-supply— India— Congresses.
Water-supply engineers— Great Britain— Biography.
Water-towers.
Water-wheels.

Power (Christian theology)
Power (Mechanics)
Power (Philosophy)
Power (Social sciences)
Power (Theology).
      SEARCH: Power (Christian theology)
Power amplifiers.
Power electronics.
Power of attorney.
Power resources.
Power spectra.

United States— History— Colonial period, ca. 1600–1775.
United States— History— Revolution, 1775–1783.
United States— History— 1815–1861.
United States— History— Civil War, 1861–1865.
United States— History— 1969–

Contrast the above examples with those below, which show the same headings arranged alphabetically, without regard for subdivisions, qualifiers, types of heading, etc.

The following examples are drawn from existing online public access catalogs rather than from the ALA filing rules:

Water— Abstracts.
Water— Aeration.
Water— Aeration— Congresses.
Water beds (Furniture)
Water— Bibliography.
Water buffalo.
Water— California— Congresses.
Water clocks.
Water— Congresses.
Water conservation— Kansas.
Water— Dictionaries.
Water districts.
Water— Economic aspects.
Water ferns.
Water— Great Lakes Region.
Water hammer.
Water— Handbooks, manuals, etc.
Water in agriculture.
Water— Law and legislation— Italy.
Water-meters.
Water pollution control industry.
Water— Pollution— Nevada.
Water quality— Pennsylvania— Philadelphia.
Water repellents.
Water resources development— California.
Water skiing.
Water softening sludge.
Water spirits in literature.
Water— Study guides.
Water-supply— California.
Water-supply engineers— Great Britain—
    Biography.
Water-supply— India— Congresses.
Water-towers.
Water— Translations from Russian.
Water-wheels.

Power amplifiers.
Power (Christian theology)
Power electronics.

Power (Mechanics)
Power of attorney.
Power (Philosophy)
Power resources.
Power (Social sciences)
Power spectra.
Power (Theology)
     SEARCH: Power (Christian theology)

United States—History—1815–1861.
United States—History—1969–
United States—History—Civil War, 1861–1865.
United States—History—Colonial period, ca. 1600–1775.
United States—History—Revolution, 1775–1783.

Note: In evaluating the above examples and all examples in the guide, it should be remembered that the examples are condensations of displays that will take up many screens in a system of any size.

Arguments in Favor of the Structured Approach

The following arguments have been made in favor of structured arrangements. Examples in these arguments are largely taken from the above set of subject heading examples:

1. Under the structured approach, the user who is interested in water alone, not in water beds, water buffalo or water skiing, can find all works on water grouped together and subarranged by form, geography or subtopic.
2. The structured approach allows the arrangement of headings to vary based on the situation. For example, history headings can be arranged chronologically, thus better matching user expectations in this discipline.
3. The structured approach, in which subdivisions (e.g.,—"Bibliography") and qualifiers (e.g., "(Theology)") are used only for subarrangement, allows users to recognize and choose applicable subdivisions or qualifiers without knowing about them

ahead of time. Subdivisions and qualifiers were designed to help the user who might not realize how
many books there are on the subject sought. Subdivisions and qualifiers function to break up a huge
list of documents into manageable subcategories, so
that a user can scan through a large list more
quickly and choose the subcategories most likely to
be useful. Depending on the information needed, a
user might decide that a dictionary would be the
most likely source of information, or that his or her
interest was mainly in the state of California, or that
the concept of power in the field of the social sciences is the one desired, not the concept of power in
the field of mechanics, etc.

In catalog technologies used prior to the advent
of online catalogs, the user was not required to specify subdivisions or qualifiers in the initial search;
these appeared once the user got to the main heading in order to aid further decision-making. When
the subdivisions and qualifiers of a heading are filed
strictly alphabetically, the user *is* required to know
of the existence of subdivisions and qualifiers in order to find the subject desired; the subdivision or
qualifier determines where the subject can be found
in what is often a multiscreen list. For example, in
the strict alphabetical arrangement, the heading
"Water—Handbooks, manuals, etc." is buried halfway down the list of headings beginning with the
term "Water"; in a system of any size, this heading
would be many screens away from the heading
"Water" with no subdivisions. The user who does not
realize that manuals are included in this subdivision
may expect to find manuals under the main heading
("Water"), or even under "Water—Manuals," and may
miss the other heading entirely in scanning through
an extremely long list.

Subdivisions and qualifiers are fabricated by catalogers at the Library of Congress; users are not expected to have them in mind prior to searching, but
only to be able to recognize and choose among them.
For example, the date spans for historical periods
used in chronological subdivisions under historical
subject headings can be somewhat arbitrary, and in

fact sometimes arouse complaints from subject experts.[3] They may very well be unfamiliar to undergraduates, scholars in other fields, and some users of public libraries, etc. Chronological arrangement at least has the benefit of making such subdivisions self-explanatory. If these subdivisions are alphabetically arranged, rather than chronologically arranged, they are likely never to be found by many users. Many other subdivisions are "free-floating": catalogers may add free-floating subdivisions to any subject heading. But free-floating subdivisions do not appear in the published *LCSH* used by many searchers to determine which subject heading to look under. The user discovers these free-floating subdivisions only on encountering them in the catalog and cannot be expected to know about them prior to that time. It is the rare user, indeed, who consults the Library of Congress subject cataloging manual before consulting the catalog![4] However, it is only there that the hapless user will find lists of free-floating subdivisions and rules about which headings they can be applied to. In general, strict alphabetical arrangement of headings with subdivisions and qualifiers has the effect of requiring users to know about artificial constructions created by catalogers.

4. Proponents of strict alphabetical arrangement argue that keyword searching obviates the need for concern about arrangement of headings, because subjects are automatically brought together by keyword matches of user requests. However, even in systems with keyword searching, multiple headings that are retrieved must be arranged in some way, preferably in some immediately discernible order. For example, the user who searches on the keyword "water" is likely to retrieve more than a screenful of headings on most systems. The frequency with which users' subject searches retrieve more than one screen of headings may be high. One research study that investigated this question reported that for 90 percent of user-input headings matched in a particular online system, there were additional headings with further subdivisions in the system.[5] It would be useful to have studies of other systems of various sizes

to compare with this one, because many of the arguments for and against structured arrangements rest on assumptions about the frequency with which users must scan through more than one screen of headings on keyword searchable systems. We know that one of the problems users reported in the Council for Library Resources (CLR) study was that of high retrieval postings.[6]

5. Online catalogs and more sophisticated programming offer the power to make structured arrangements comprehensible to users without requiring them to know complex filing rules. For example, shorter initial displays could show headings without subdivisions and subdivisions could be shown only after a particular heading is chosen; node labels could be used to organize displays, e.g., "By historical period" or "By geographic area"; online messages could be used to explain, e.g., that headings are arranged first chronologically, then by topic, then by geographic area; and boldface, blinking text, color, and other graphic elements could be used to better explicate the organization of structured displays. Several writers have suggested the use of compression techniques based on logical categories to reduce long displays.[7]

6. The *Library of Congress Subject Headings (LCSH)* and *Medical Subject Headings (MeSH)* are highly structured subject heading strings designed to be arranged in a structured way, as they are arranged in the systems used at the Library of Congress and the National Library of Medicine. Catalogers at the Library of Congress and the National Library of Medicine and libraries that follow their cataloging practices spend time and effort every day building structure into new headings. MARC format tags and subfields were designed to support structured arrangements; they would be considerably less complex if they were designed to support only a strict alphabetical arrangement. If no one is using these structured headings to create structured displays, all of the effort invested in creating this complexity is wasted. Also, the complexity of headings designed for structured displays is confusing for users when the

headings are arranged in alphabetical order instead. As John Rather and Susan Biebel state in *Library of Congress Filing Rules* (1980), "It is illogical to construct a heading one way, and then to file it as if it were constructed another way." (p. 2)

7. Many libraries make the printed volumes of *LCSH* or *LCSH* on CD-ROM available to users to aid in the choice of subject headings. Headings in the printed volumes and on CD-ROM are arranged in a structured fashion. User experience with the arrangement in the printed volumes and CD-ROM might create expectations contrary to what is found in the catalog, if the catalog is arranged alphabetically.

8. Arguments that the added costs of programming and supporting structured arrangements in online systems are not worth what is gained may be met with the following counter-arguments:

   a) The costs associated with more complex programming may be justified because users befuddled by strict alphabetical arrangements spend more time in searching.

   b) Systems on CD-ROM or minicomputers would not be burdened with ongoing input/output costs that may be accrued on mainframe systems for complex sorting programs and the like.

   c) It is unfair to place the burden of searching through long displays on the user rather than on the computer.

Arguments in Favor of the Strict Alphabetical Approach

The following are arguments that have been made in favor of alphabetical arrangements:

1. Strict alphabetical arrangement is simple and straightforward. A single rule covers all situations: Subject headings are arranged word by word, disregarding punctuation. Once users learn this simple rule, those who know the heading they are seeking

will not become lost in a sometimes inscrutable structured arrangement.

2. Programming of sorting rules for strict alphabetical arrangement is simpler and less costly. If sorting is done at the time the results of a search are displayed, complex sorting rules can degrade system performance; if presorting is done, complex sorting rules have an adverse impact on online real time updating of the database.

3. When a keyword search retrieves less than a screenful of headings, the arrangement of those headings is irrelevant; the user can easily scan them all.

4. *LCSH* is notoriously inconsistent in its structuring. For example, it contains both the heading "Water—Pollution" and the heading "Water quality." In a strict alphabetical arrangement, the user who expects to find the heading "Water pollution" will find "Water—Pollution" in the same place.

Concluding Remarks

Although arguments may be made in favor of or against pure structured arrangements or strict alphabetical arrangements, the decisions made by individual libraries or systems need not be absolute. For example, a library that for the most part favors strict alphabetical arrangement may decide to disregard parenthetical qualifiers in the arrangement of headings or to arrange chronological subdivisions chronologically. System designers and librarians grappling with arrangement issues may well decide to make separate decisions about the options presented on the following pages.

Collection size and type of library may be a factor in decision-making. User searches of an online catalog in a small library may produce multiple-screen displays much less frequently than the same searches in a large research library. It may be argued that some structured arrangements are more readily comprehensible to highly educated users or to very experienced library users (although this argument should be examined carefully and probably does not hold true in cases such as the chronological arrangement of chronological subdivisions, which probably meets user expectations in all types of libraries).

The important thing to remember in designing displays is that one should never assume users of the catalog know the subject heading they need prior to the search; systems should be designed to encourage exploration and to teach structure by example.

Acknowledgments

The Subcommittee received a great deal of help from many individuals. Allyson Carlyle wrote several drafts of the introduction and Jane Magree edited the examples extensively; both had many useful criticisms and suggestions regarding the document as a whole. Mary K. Pietris always made time for our meetings and was always ready to enlist her remarkable memory and her considerable experience in contributing the most illuminating example to any particular discussion. Many people put in considerable time studying existing systems and identifying problems for us; among them Kathryn Bading, Julianne Beall, Barbara Berman, Lois Mai Chan, Bill Garrison, Bob Ihrig, Cecilia Knight, Lois Pausch, Alan Pochi, Avi Rappoport, May C. Rathbone, and Mark Watson. Other people who faithfully attended meetings, served as liaisons to other committees, and made helpful suggestions that improved the guide include Karen Calhoun, Sandy Heft, Mary Charles Lasater, Sara Shatford Layne, Peter Lisbon, Winton Matthews, Dorothy McGarry, James J. Michael, Gregory New, Barbara Orbach, Margaret Rohdy, Steve Salmon, Barbara Strauss, Elaine Svenonius, and Paul Weiss. Robert P. Holley's work on the problems with computer arrangement of chronological subdivisions was a strong stimulus for the creation of the Subcommittee and a solid foundation for its work. Carolyn Mueller, David Gleim, and Karen Muller helped shepherd the guide through the ALA publication process with great efficiency. The Subcommittee would like to give our special thanks to the system designers who turned out from 8 to 10 on a Monday evening at the 1991 Midwinter Meeting to give us encouragement and detailed help with the guide; the enthusiasm with which the system designers greeted our efforts leads us to believe that more forums are needed to encourage discussion among those whose decisions affect the design of online public access catalogs, catalogers, and system designers alike.

Notes

1. *Library of Congress Filing Rules*, prepared by John C. Rather and Susan C. Biebel (Washington: Library of Congress, 1980).

2. *ALA Filing Rules*, Filing Committee, Resources and Technical Services Division, American Library Association (Chicago: American Library Association, 1980).

3. See for example: John McKinlay, "Australia, LCSH an FLASH," *Library Resources & Technical Services* 26:2 (April/June 1982): 105; Meng-Fen Su, "On Cataloging and Classifying Chinese History," *Cataloging & Classification Quarterly* 4:2 (Winter 1983): 51–71.

4. Library of Congress. Subject Cataloging Division. *Subject Cataloging Manual: Subject Headings*, 3rd ed. (Washington, D.C.: Library of Congress, 1988).

5. Noelle Van Pulis and Lorene E. Ludy, "Subject Searching in an Online Catalog with Authority Control," *College & Research Libraries* 49:6 (Nov. 1988): 529.

6. For example, see *Using Online Catalogs: A Nationwide Survey*, edited by Joseph R. Matthews, Gary S. Lawrence, and Douglas K. Ferguson (New York: Neal-Schuman, 1983): 124.

7. Karen Markey Drabenstott and Diane Vizine-Goetz, "Search Trees for Subject Searching in Online Catalogs," *Library Hi Tech* 31 (1990, no. 3): 7–20; Dorothy McGarry and Elaine Svenonius, "More on Improved Browsable Displays for Online Subject Access," *Information Technology and Libraries* 10:3 (Sept. 1991): 185–91; Mia Massicotte, "Improved Browsable Displays for Online Subject Access," *Information Technology and Libraries* 7:4 (1988): 373–80.

I. Display of Subdivisions

▬▬▬ ▪▪ ▬▬ ▪▪ ▬▬

A. Display of Subdivisions under the Main Heading to Which They Are Attached

Should subdivisions display under the main heading to which they are attached (method 1, LC filing rules), or should they display among other longer main headings (method 2, ALA filing rules)?

EXAMPLES

Method 1

Water— Abstracts.
Water— Aeration.
Water— Aeration—
   Congresses.
Water— Bibliography.
Water— California—
   Congresses.
Water— Congresses.
Water— Dictionaries.
Water— Economic
   aspects.
Water— Great Lakes
   Region.

Method 2

Water— Abstracts.
Water— Aeration.
Water— Aeration— Congresses.
Water beds (Furniture)
Water— Bibliography.
Water buffalo.
Water— California— Congresses.
Water clocks.
Water— Congresses.
Water conservation— Kansas.

Method 1 (continued)

Water— Handbooks, manuals, etc.

Water— Law and legislation— Italy.

Water— Pollution— Nevada.

Water— Study guides.

Water— Translations from Russian.

Water— United States— Congresses.

Water beds (Furniture)

Water buffalo.

Water clocks.

Water conservation— Kansas.

Water districts.

Water ferns.

Water hammer.

Water in agriculture.

Water-meters.

Water pollution control industry.

Water quality— Pennsylvania— Philadelphia.

Water repellents.

Water resources development— California.

Water skiing.

Water softening sludge.

Water spirits in literature.

Water-supply— California.

Water-supply— India— Congresses.

Water-supply engineers— Great Britain— Biography.

Water-towers.

Water-wheels.

Method 2 (continued)

Water— Dictionaries.

Water districts.

Water— Economic aspects.

Water ferns.

Water— Great Lakes Region.

Water hammer.

Water— Handbooks, manuals, etc.

Water in agriculture.

Water— Law and legislation— Italy.

Water-meters.

Water pollution control industry.

Water— Pollution— Nevada.

Water quality— Pennsylvania— Philadelphia.

Water repellents.

Water resources development— California.

Water skiing.

Water softening sludge.

Water spirits in literature.

Water— Study guides.

Water-supply— California.

Water-supply engineers— Great Britain— Biography.

Water-supply— India— Congresses.

Water-towers.

Water— Translations from Russian.

Water-wheels.

CURRENT PRACTICE

ALA filing rules, rule 1, p. 9, recommend following method 2; LC filing rules, rule 5.7, p. 34, recommend following method 1. Existing systems follow both methods.

PROs AND CONs

A user looking for a book about water might not realize how many books there are to be found. The subdivisions function to break up a huge file into manageable subcategories so that a user can scan through a large file more quickly and make choices as to the subcategories most likely to be useful. Depending on the information needed, a user might decide that a dictionary would be the most likely source of information, or that his or her interest was mainly in the state of California, etc. In the catalog technologies that preceded online catalogs (card and book catalogs), the user was not required to specify subdivisions in the initial search; the subdivisions appeared once the user got to the main heading in order to aid further decision-making. The heading-subdivision approach was not designed for systems that require a user to type in an exact match, letter by letter, before being shown what choices are available.

Under method 1, the user who is interested in water alone, not in water beds, water buffalo or water skiing, can find all works on water grouped together and subarranged by form, geography, or subtopic. This method is less successful in cases where LC has created a topical subdivision for a concept that could be expressed in an adjectival main heading. For example, a user might quite reasonably expect to find the subdivided heading "Water—Aeration" under the adjectival main heading "Water Aeration," following the pattern of the adjectival heading "Water Conservation."

Under method 2, the user interested in "water" will have a much harder time locating the desired information. Dozens of screens could separate one subdivision under "Water" from another. The user is required to know more about subdivision practice in order to find useful materials. "Water—Handbooks, manuals, etc.," for example, is buried halfway down the list of headings beginning with the term "Water"; in a system of any size, this heading would be many screens away from the heading "Water" with no subdivisions. The user who does not realize that manuals are accessed by means of this subdivision may expect to find manuals under the main heading ("Water"), or even under "Water—Manuals," and may miss the other heading entirely in scanning through an extremely long list. In favor of method 2, the user who is seeking "Water Aeration," following the pattern of "Water Conservation," may be more likely to notice it under method 2.

B. Heading-Subdivision Combinations That Are Identical

Should all heading-subdivision combinations that are identical display together (method 1, LC filing rules) or should they display among other longer heading-subdivision combinations (method 2, ALA filing rules)?

EXAMPLES

Method 1

United States—History— Drama.
United States—History— Sources.
United States—History, Military.

Method 2

United States—History—Drama.
United States—History, Military.
United States—History— Sources.

CURRENT PRACTICE

ALA filing rules, rule 1, recommend following method 2; LC filing rules, rule 3.3.5, and rule 7.2, recommend following method 1. Existing systems follow both methods.

PROs AND CONs

This problem is not conceptually different from the problem of whether or not to group main headings together before subarranging by subdivision; here the question is whether or not first subdivisions should be grouped together before subarranging by subsequent subdivisions. We included a separate section on this problem, rather than subsuming it under I.A. above, to ensure that system designers were aware that the problem occurs with pieces of the heading that occur after the main heading.

Under method 1, the user who is interested only in general U.S. history, not in military history of the United States, can find materials of interest grouped together, not scattered among or fragmented by materials on more specific types of history. For this method to work, however, users must notice that like subdivisions are grouped together before being subarranged by subsequent subdivisions.

C. Order of Chronological Subdivisions

Should chronological subdivisions display in chronological order, regardless of whether or not they begin with numerals (method 1, LC and ALA filing rules), or should they display in alphabetical order (method 2)?

EXAMPLES

Method 1

United States—
    History— Colonial
    period, ca. 1600–1775.
United States—
    History— Revolution,
    1775–1783.
United States—
    History— 1815–1861.
United States—
    History— Civil War,
    1861–1865.
United States—
    History— 1969–

Method 2

United States— History—
    1815–1861.
United States— History— 1969–
United States— History—
    Civil War, 1861–1865.
United States— History—
    Colonial period,
    ca. 1600–1775.
United States— History—
    Revolution, 1775–1783.

CURRENT PRACTICE

ALA filing rules, rule 8.7.2, and LC filing rules, rule 16.7.1, both recommend method 1. Only one existing system follows method 1; all others follow method 2. (Please note the warning in the introduction that observations of current systems practice in this guide do not constitute any sort of standard or better way of doing things.)

PROs AND CONs

No arguments in favor of method 2 can be advanced, other than those of lower cost and more programming simplicity. It is generally agreed that chronological arrangement of chronological subdivisions is better for users. Unfortunately, most current online public access catalogs do not arrange chronologically those subdivisions that begin with alphabetic characters, as in the Civil War example above. Users are likely to find one chronological sequence in the file and look no further, not realizing that chronological headings are arranged in several sequences, depending on whether or not the subdivision begins with alphabetic characters. A number of solutions can be envisioned. Chronological subdivisions are given a different subfield code (≠y) in the MARC format; this could be used to devise smart sort programs that could skip alphabetic characters and look for the first numeric ones. If this method is considered too complex and costly, chronological subdivisions could be machine-manipulated to rotate the numeric characters to the beginning of the subdivision permanently, as suggested years ago by Lois Mai Chan[1]; this could be done to the records either at the national level or at the time of loading them into the local system. At any rate, this is an area where clever programming could help considerably to ease the user's path through our complex systems.

D. Chronological Subdivisions with Three Numeral Dates

Should three numeral dates be arranged before four numeral dates (method 1, LC and ALA filing rules) or should standard computer sorting of numerals be used (method 2)?

EXAMPLES

Method 1

Rome (Italy)— History—
476-1420.
Rome (Italy)— History—
1420-1798.

Method 2

Rome (Italy)— History—
1420-1798.
Rome (Italy)— History—
476-1420.

CURRENT PRACTICE

ALA filing rules, rule 8.1, and LC filing rules, rule 16, both call for displaying numerals in ascending order according to their numerical value. Some current systems follow method 1 and some follow method 2; method 2 may represent the default in most systems if programming is not done to overcome it.

PROs AND CONs

Every effort should be made in online public access catalogs to override standard computer numeral sort programs and arrange numerals in chronological subdivisions in ascending numerical order, because the latter order meets user expectations. (See also section IVC on ascending numerical order.)

E. Chronological Subdivisions for Centuries

Should chronological subdivisions for centuries be arranged as if they were expressed in a numerical range, e.g., 19th century arranged as if it were 1801-1900 as in the LC filing rules, or 1800-1899 as in the ALA filing rules (either of which constitutes method 1), or arranged as written (method 2)?

EXAMPLES

Method 1

China— History— Ch'ien-
lung, 1736-1795.

Method 2

China— History— Ch'ien-lung,
1736-1795.

Method 1 (continued)

China— History—
   19th century.
China— History— Opium
   War of 1840–1842.
China— History—
   1861–1912.
China— History—
   1928–1937.

Method 2 (continued)

China— Historv— Opium War of
   1840–1842.
China— History— 1861–1912.
China— History— 19th century.
China— History— 1928–1937.

CURRENT PRACTICE

ALA filing rules, rule 8.7.2, page 34, and LC filing rules, rule 16.7.1, page 72, both recommend method 1. No existing systems follow method 1. (Please note the warning in the introduction that observations of current systems practice do not constitute any sort of standard or better way of doing things.)

PROs AND CONs

Following the filing rules and arranging chronological subdivisions for centuries as if they were expressed in a numerical range (method 1) contributes to keeping the chronological arrangement logical, orderly, and predictable for users. Unfortunately, arranging headings as if they were different from what they are requires complex programming; no existing systems that we know of have done this programming. Filing factors that are not apparent can also cause confusion to users. It would be helpful if cross-references could be made from the date expressed as a range to the subdivision for the century. However, such a solution would require a change in the current LC policy of not creating and distributing authority records for subdivisions, and local systems would have to change their applications to deal with authority records for subdivisions.

F. Chronological Subdivisions for B.C. Dates

Should chronological subdivisions for B.C. dates be arranged in inverse numerical order before all A.D. dates (method 1, LC and ALA filing rules) or should they be in-terfiled with A.D. dates in ascending numerical order (method 2)?

EXAMPLES

Method 1

Rome— History— Republic, 265–30 B.C.

Rome— History— Servile Wars, 135–71 B.C.

Rome— History— Conspiracy of Catiline, 65–62 B.C.

Rome— History— Nero, 54–68.

Rome— History— Antoninus Pius, 138–161.

Rome— History— Claudius II, 268–270?

Method 2

Rome— History— Nero, 54–68.

Rome— History— Conspiracy of Catiline, 65–62 B.C.

Rome— History— Servile Wars, 135–71 B.C.

Rome— History— Antoninus Pius, 138–161.

Rome— History— Republic, 265–30 B.C.

Rome— History— Claudius II, 268–270?

CURRENT PRACTICE

ALA filing rules, rule 8.7.1, p. 34, and LC filing rules, rule 16.7, p. 72, both recommend method 1. No existing systems follow method 1, probably because of the complexity of the possible programming solution.

PROs AND CONs

Once again, method 1 is recommended by both sets of filing rules for a logical, predictable, readily recognizable or-dering. However, no current online systems employ this method, undoubtedly because it would require complex sorting programs. A smart program that could recognize the B.C. and act accordingly, e.g., arrange the following num-ber as if it were a negative number, can be envisioned.

G. Chronological Subdivisions with a Date Span

If two chronological subdivisions include a date span, each of which begins with the same date, should the entry which represents the shorter time span be arranged first (method 1, LC and ALA filing rules), or second (method 2)? If an open-ended date must be arranged with the spans, should it be arranged before a closed date span (method 3, ALA filing rules), or after it (method 4, LC filing rules)?

EXAMPLES

Method 1

United States— History— 1865–1898.
United States— History— 1865–1921.

Method 2

United States— History— 1865–1921.
United States— History— 1865–1898.

Method 3

United States— History— 1865–
United States— History— 1865–1898.
United States— History— 1865–1921.

Method 4

United States— History— 1865–1898.
United States— History— 1865–1921.
United States— History— 1865–

CURRENT PRACTICE

ALA filing rules show methods 1 and 3 in the example under rule 8.7.2, p. 35. LC filing rules specify methods 1 and 4 in rule 16.7, p. 72–73. Most online systems follow method 1.

PROs AND CONs

A strictly numerical sequence as favored by the ALA and LC filing rules and by most online catalogs will probably lead to less user confusion in understanding the arrangement. In the case of open-ended dates, a strictly numerical sequence may not present the subject matter in the best order for the user.

H. Chronological Subdivisions in the Form of "To [Date]"

Should a chronological subdivision in the form of "To [date]" be arranged as if it read "0–[date]" (method 1, ALA and LC filing rules), or strictly alphabetically (method 2)?

EXAMPLES

Method 1

Egypt— History— To 332 B.C.
Egypt— History— To 640 A.D.
Egypt— History—
  332–30 B.C.
Egypt— History— 30 B.C.–
  640 A.D.
Egypt— History—
  640–1250.
Egypt— History— 1798–

Method 2

Egypt— History— 332–30 B.C.
Egypt— History— 30 B.C.–
  640 A.D.
Egypt— History— 640–1250.
Egypt— History— 1798–
Egypt— History— To 332 B.C.
Egypt— History— To 640 A.D.

CURRENT PRACTICE

ALA filing rules, rule 8.7.2, p. 34, and LC filing rules, rule 16.7.1, p. 72, both recommend method 1. No existing systems use method 1, probably because of the complexity of the sorting program that would be required. Note: Existing filing rules do not indicate explicitly how several "To" date subdivisions should be arranged, although examples appear to indicate that the earliest ending date should come before the later ones; for example, "To 600 B.C." should come before "To 300 A.D."

PROs AND CONs

Unfortunately, current online catalogs follow method 2. Such an arrangement may cause a problem for the browsing user who may not realize that the earliest period is out of chronological sequence. On the other hand, the user might be confused by the transparency of the "To" in method 1.

I. Topical, Geographical, and Chronological Subdivisions

Should topical subdivisions display separately from geographical and chronological subdivisions (method 1, LC filing rules) or should all subdivisions display in one single alphabetic order (method 2, ALA filing rules)?

Examples

Method 1

Economic history—
1600–1750.
Economic history—
1945–1971.
Economic history— 1971–
Economic history—
Abstracts.
Economic history—
Bibliography.
Economic history—
Dictionaries— Chinese.
Economic history— Library
resources.
Economic history—
Research.
Economic history—
Statistics.
Economic history— Africa.
Economic history— Africa,
West.
Economic history—
California—
San Francisco.
Economic history—
Germany.
Economic history—
Oklahoma— Tulsa.
Economic history—
Russian S.F.S.R.—
Moscow.
Economic history—
Ukraine— Kiev.

United States— History—
Colonial period,
ca. 1600–1775.
United States— History—
King William's
War, 1689–1697.
United States— History—
War of 1812.

Method 2

Economic history— 1600–1750.
Economic history— 1945–1971.
Economic history— 1971–
Economic history— Abstracts.
Economic history— Africa.
Economic history— Africa, West.
Economic history— Bibliography.
Economic history— California—
San Francisco.
Economic history—
Dictionaries— Chinese.
Economic history— Germany.
Economic history— Library
resources.
Economic history— Oklahoma—
Tulsa.
Economic history— Research.
Economic history— Russian
S.F.S.R.— Moscow.
Economic history— Statistics.
Economic history— Ukraine—
Kiev.

United States— History—
1933–1945.
United States— History—
Anecdotes.
United States— History—
Colonial period,
ca. 1600–1775.
United States— History—
Dictionaries.
United States— History— King
William's War, 1689–1697.
United States— History— Study
and teaching.
United States— History—
War of 1812.

Method 1 (continued)

United States—History—
    1933–1945.
United States—History—
    Anecdotes.
United States—History—
    Dictionaries.
United States—History—
    Study and teaching.

CURRENT PRACTICE

ALA filing rules, rule 1, recommend following method 2; LC filing rules, rule 5.8, recommend that subdivisions be grouped in the following order: 1) period subdivisions, 2) form and topical subdivisions, and 3) geographical subdivisions. Only two existing systems follow method 1; all others follow method 2.

PROs AND CONs

Method 1 allows those users who know their primary interest in a subject is chronological or geographical to scan through just the chronological or geographical subdivisions, unimpeded by other types of subdivision. This could be helpful to users who do not know geographical or chronological subdivision practice. For example, the user interested in Tulsa who does not know whether to look under "T" for Tulsa, "U" for United States or "O" for Oklahoma will have fewer headings to scan through. This advantage is gained only at the price of requiring the user to learn more about how the system works, however. The unwary user may fail to notice that a logical classification, rather than strict alphabetical order, is being employed. Any system that employs method 1 should clearly inform users that strict alphabetical order is not being followed. It might be helpful to put chronological and geographical subdivisions first, with a screen message to users that subjects are listed first by date or by place, and then by topic. Alternatively, placing these subdivisions at the end should be considered, with a screen message that materials on the subject at a particular date or in a particular place are listed at the end.

It should be noted that the classification of geographical and chronological subdivisions in displays is not the only method of allowing users ready access to these aspects of a subject. The differentiation among these different types of subdivision in MARC format subfield coding could allow systems to query users interested in a subject as to whether they were interested in seeing works arranged by period or by geographic area. System designers might want to experiment with prompts or limit searches that allow a user to specifically request the geographical subdivisions only or the chronological subdivisions only; messages that allow users to find these subdivisions quickly in long displays; or node labels such as "By historical period" or "By geographical area."

Some may feel that it would be useful to group form subdivisions together. Examples of form subdivisions are "Dictionaries" and "Handbooks, manuals, etc." Unfortunately, *LCSH* does not now identify form subdivisions as distinct from topical subdivisions, nor does the MARC format have a different subfield code to distinguish form from topical subdivisions. *MeSH* does clearly distinguish form from topical subdivisions, but the lack of a MARC subfield code would necessitate local programming and/or cataloging solutions to identify *MeSH* form subdivisions for display purposes.

J. Mechanically Defined Order of Subdivisions

Highly undesirable results are obtained if a system displays the subdivisions attached to a single heading in an order based on the MARC subfield code; an example of such mechanically defined order might be: ≠x subfields always precede ≠y subfields, which always precede ≠z subfields. The subcommittee recommends that no system follow this practice, because it changes the meaning of headings. For example, the heading "Agriculture— United States— Research" refers to agriculture in the United States; the heading "Agriculture— Research— United States" refers to research done in the United States. The order of subfields should be left to the discretion of the cataloger so that the subject of the work is clearly conveyed to the user, and so that the optimum arrangement of subdivisions under any given subject may be employed.

EXAMPLE

Heading input by cataloger:
Popular music— Germany— 1921–1930.

Heading manipulated by machine:
Popular music— 1921–1930— Germany.

II. Inverted Headings

Should inverted headings display before longer phrase headings (method 1, LC filing rules), among longer phrase headings (method 2, ALA filing rules), or after longer phrase headings (method 3)?

EXAMPLES

Method 1	Method 2	Method 3
Art.	Art.	Art.
Art, American.	Art, American.	Art as an investment.
Art, Celtic.	Art as an investment.	Art calendars.
Art, Croatian.	Art calendars.	Art centers.
Art, Modern.	Art, Celtic.	Art deco.
Art, Tantric.	Art centers.	Art previews.
Art, Victorian.	Art, Croatian.	Art thefts.
Art as an investment.	Art deco.	Art, American.
Art calendars.	Art, Modern.	Art, Celtic.
Art centers.	Art previews.	Art, Croatian.
Art deco.	Art, Tantric.	Art, Modern.
Art previews.	Art thefts.	Art, Tantric.
Art thefts.	Art, Victorian.	Art, Victorian.

CURRENT PRACTICE

ALA filing rules, rule 1, recommend following method 2; LC filing rules, rule 5.7, recommend following method 1. No existing online systems follow method 1. Most follow method 2, but some follow method 3.

PROs AND CONs

Inversion serves as a kind of subdivision. Thus, the same arguments made in favor of keeping all subdivisions together under the main heading can be made in favor of keeping inverted headings together in front of longer phrase headings (method 1). Method 1 favors the user who, for example, is interested only in art *per se,* not in art calendars, art thefts, etc. In this particular case, the inverted headings are very similar to headings with geographical subdivisions.

The disadvantage is the same as in all violations of strict alphabetical order: the user must be warned about the fact that strict alphabetical order is not being followed.

In order to follow method 1, the system must be designed to differentiate between significant commas and insignificant commas. An example of an insignificant comma is found in the heading "Piano, Flute, Viola with string orchestra." An example of a significant comma is found in the heading "Art, African." The Library of Congress recommends that the following rule be applied to topical subject headings *only*(!): a comma followed by an upper-case letter is significant; when the following letter is lowercase, the comma is insignificant (LC filing rules, p. 22).

III. Display of Qualified Headings

Should qualified headings display before longer phrase headings (method 1, LC filing rules), or among other longer phrase headings (method 2, ALA filing rules)?

EXAMPLES

Method 1

Power (Christian
   theology)
Power (Mechanics)
Power (Philosophy)
Power (Social sciences)
Power (Theology)
   SEARCH: Power
   (Christian theology)
Power amplifiers.
Power electronics.
Power of attorney.
Power resources.
Power spectra.

Method 2

Power amplifiers.
Power (Christian theology)
Power electronics.
Power (Mechanics)
Power of attorney.
Power (Philosophy)
Power resources.
Power (Social sciences)
Power spectra.
Power (Theology)
   SEARCH: Power
   (Christian theology)

CURRENT PRACTICE

ALA filing rules, rule 1, recommend following method 2; LC filing rules, rule 5.7, recommend following method 1. Only three existing systems have done the programming necessary to arrange such headings according to method 1.

PROs AND CONs

The parenthetical qualifier is used in both descriptive and subject cataloging when a term or a name could refer to more than one concept or entity, and something is needed to warn users of this fact, and to allow users to choose which of several concepts or entities they are interested in. For example, a political scientist may decide to do research on "power," and not consider the fact that the library may have many works that use the term "power" the way an engineer or a theologian would. Catalogers use parenthetical qualifiers to allow the user to choose. It was never intended that users be able to specify the qualifier ahead of time; the qualifiers were meant to appear once the user got to the heading in order to aid further decision-making. Our hypothetical political scientist who does a search using the term "power" should be presented with the following display:

> Power (Christian theology)
> Power (Mechanics)
> Power (Philosophy)
> Power (Social sciences)

Grouping qualified headings together before longer phrase headings, as in method 1, ensures that the user will be presented with this choice. In method 2, in a file of any size, the political scientist may fail to find the correct heading at all. It is recommended that all systems ignore parenthetical qualifiers in initial sorting, using them only for subarrangement.

Note 1: Some normalization programs eliminate parentheses before sorting; an example is the normalization program used by the Linked Systems Project (LSP). It is imperative either that these normalization programs be changed, or that the MARC format be changed to allow for subfield coding of parenthetical qualifiers. Our systems should never require users to know of the existence of an artificial, constructed parenthetical qualifier in order to find a heading.

Note 2: When both inverted and qualified headings must be interfiled, the LC filing rules, rule 5.7, call for the following order:

    Children.
    Children— Surgery.
    Children, Adopted.
    Children, Vagrant.
    Children (International law)
    Children (Roman law)
    Children as authors.

Some would argue that since inverted headings are more like longer phrase headings— only inverted— they ought to come after qualified headings. Others would argue that the inverted part of an inverted heading is very like a qualifier in disguise, in which case perhaps inverted headings should be interfiled with qualified headings.

IV. Arrangement of Numerical Headings

A. Numbers and Letters

Should numbers display before letters (method 1, LC and ALA filing rules), after letters (method 2), as if they were spelled out (method 3), or, if spelled out, as if they were numerals (method 4)?

EXAMPLES

Method 1

4-H clubs.
35mm cameras.
97 Sen (Fighter planes)
109/b (Computer)
Fountain pens.
Fourth of July.
Nightmares.
Ninety-nine (Game)
One (The number)
Orange juice.
Thatched roofs.
Thirteen (The number)
Thirty-five hour week.
Towels.

Method 2

Fountain pens.
Fourth of July.
Nightmares.
Ninety-nine (Game)
One (The number)
Orange juice.
Thatched roofs.
Thirteen (The number)
Thirty-five hour week.
Towels.
4-H clubs.
35mm cameras.
97 Sen (Fighter planes)
109/b (Computer)

Method 3

Fountain pens.
4-H clubs.
Fourth of July.
Nightmares.
Ninety-nine (Game)
97 Sen (Fighter planes)
One (The number)
109/b (Computer)
Orange juice.
Thatched roofs.
Thirteen (The number)
Thirty-five hour week.
35mm cameras.
Towels.

Method 4

One (The number)
4-H clubs.
Fourth of July.
Thirteen (The number)
Thirty-five hour week.
35mm cameras.
97 Sen (Fighter planes)
Ninety-nine (Game)
109/b (Computer)
Fountain pens.
Nightmares.
Orange juice.
Thatched roofs.
Towels.

CURRENT PRACTICE

ALA filing rules, rule 1, and LC filing rules, rule 1.2 and rule 16 (detailed), both recommend following method 1. Most online systems follow method 1, with a few following method 2.

PROs AND CONs

Users have no way of knowing whether catalogers have used the numerical or the spelled out form. Methods 1 and 2 require the user to search under both forms to be sure (and many users may not think to do this). However, method 3, in treating numbers as if they were spelled out, causes user confusion of another variety—what is the correct way to spell out a number? Is "100" spelled "a hundred" or "one hundred"? Methods 3 and 4 would both be very difficult to implement; some possible solutions might be online dictionaries, extensive explanatory cross-references, or special "arrange-as-if" fields linked to subject heading fields. If it were possible to devise a way to adopt method 4 in the computer, this method would appear to have great promise for improved displays, since it would collocate all numbers, whether they were expressed in digits or words, and would not require the user to know how catalogers have chosen to express a number. At the very least, general *see also* references from the alphabetical to the numerical representations and vice versa would be helpful; note that references from the spelled out form must specify whether numbers are to be found before or after letters to be truly helpful.

B. Roman Numerals

Should Roman numerals be arranged as letters, or as their arabic numerical equivalents (ALA and LC filing rules)?

EXAMPLES

> DNA topoisomerase I.
> DNA topoisomerase II.

CURRENT PRACTICE

ALA filing rules, rule 8.5, and LC filing rules, rule 16.2, both recommend following method 2. No current online systems seem to have devised a way of following method 2 (i.e., all, by default one suspects, follow method 1).

PROs AND CONs

It seems difficult to argue against the proposition that user expectations demand filing Roman numerals in numerical order; this is the logical and expected order. However, it is difficult to conceive of an algorithm that would allow a computer to tell the difference between a Roman numeral and the same letter used as a word. Fortunately, Roman numerals rarely occur in subject headings. Those that do are found beyond the primary filing element and are the smaller numbers, which when filed alphabetically are also filed numerically (I, II, III, IV, V, VI, VII, etc.).

C. Ascending Numerical Order

Should numbers be arranged in ascending numerical order (method 1, LC and ALA rules), or in some other order (method 2)?

EXAMPLES

Method 1

United States. Army. 15th
   Infantry.
United States. Army. 110th
   Infantry.

Method 2

United States. Army. 110th
   Infantry.
United States. Army. 15th
   Infantry.

CURRENT PRACTICE

ALA filing rules, rule 1, and LC filing rules, rule 1.2 and rule 16 (detailed), recommend following method 1. LC filing rules further stipulate that ordinal numbers file immediately after cardinal numbers of the same value (rule 16.3). Some existing systems follow method 2, but one suspects this is because it is the default when programming is not done to solve the problem.

PROs AND CONs

User expectations demand following method 1.

V. Display of Subjects Interfiled with Names and Titles

━━━ ━ ━━━ ━ ━━━

A. Same Initial Filing Element

When subject headings are displayed in one alphabet with names and titles in a dictionary arrangement, should entities with the same initial filing element[2] be filed by type of heading (method 1, LC filing rules), or interfiled alphabetically regardless of type (method 2), or should all headings be filed alphabetically word-by-word regardless of initial filing element or type of heading (method 3, ALA filing rules)?

EXAMPLES

Method 1

King.	[forename]
King, A. Hyatt (Alec Hyatt), 1911–	[surname]
King, Martin Luther, Jr., 1924–1968.	[surname]
King, Stephen, 1947–	[surname]
King (Firm)	[corporate name]
King (Musical group)	[corporate name]
King (N.C.)	[corporate name]
King (Ship)	[corporate name]
King (Tex.)	[corporate name]
King (Chess)	[topical subject]
King.	[title]

King : reminiscences.	[title]
King and country.	[title]
King-Boyes, M.J.E.	[compound surname]
King cobra.	[topical subject]
King family.	[surname]
King Herod's dream.	[title]
King mackerel.	[topical subject]
King o the black art and other folk tales.	[title]
King penguin.	[topical subject]
The King site.	[title]
The king who knew not fear.	[title]

Water.	[subject heading]
Water—Abstracts.	[subject heading]
Water—Handbooks, manuals, etc.	[subject heading]
Water.	[title]
Water [art original]	[title]
Water! [videorecording]	[title]
Water abstracts.	[title]
Water analysis.	[title]
Water and Sanitation for Health Project (U.S.)	[corporate body]

Method 2

King.	[forename]
King.	[title]
King, A. Hyatt (Alec Hyatt), 1911–	[surname]
King (Chess)	[topical subject]
King (Firm)	[corporate name]
King, Martin Luther, Jr., 1924–1968.	[surname]
King (Musical group)	[corporate name]
King (N.C.)	[corporate name]
King : reminiscences.	[title]
King (Ship)	[corporate name]
King, Stephen, 1947-	[surname]
King (Tex.)	[corporate name]
King and country.	[title]
King-Boyes, M.J.E.	[compound surname]
King cobra.	[topical subject]
King family.	[surname]
King Herod's dream.	[title]
King mackerel.	[topical subject]
King o the black art and other folk tales.	[title]
King penguin.	[topical subject]

The King site.	[title]
The king who knew not fear.	[title]
Water.	[title]
Water.	[subject heading]
Water—Abstracts.	[subject heading]
Water [art original]	[title]
Water—Handbooks, manuals, etc.	[subject heading]
Water! [videorecording]	[title]
Water abstracts.	[title]
Water analysis.	[title]
Water and Sanitation for Health Project (U.S.)	[corporate body]

Method 3

King.	[forename]
King.	[title]
King, A. Hyatt (Alec Hyatt), 1911–	[surname]
King and country.	[title]
King-Boyes, M.J.E.	[compound surname]
King (Chess)	[topical subject]
King cobra.	[topical subject]
King family.	[surname]
King (Firm)	[corporate name]
King Herod's dream.	[title]
King mackerel.	[topical subject]
King, Martin Luther, Jr., 1924–1968	[surname]
King (Musical group)	[corporate name]
King (N.C.)	[corporate name]
King o the black art and other folk tales.	[title]
King penguin.	[topical subject]
King : reminiscences.	[title]
King (Ship)	[corporate name]
The King site.	[title]
King, Stephen, 1947–	[surname]
King (Tex.)	[corporate name]
The king who knew not fear.	[title]
Water.	[title]
Water.	[subject heading]
Water abstracts.	[title]
Water—Abstracts.	[subject heading]
Water analysis.	[title]
Water and Sanitation for Health Project (U.S.)	[corporate body]
Water [art original]	[title]

Water— Handbooks, manuals, etc.   [subject heading]
Water! [videorecording]   [title]

CURRENT PRACTICE

ALA filing rules, rule 1, recommend following method 3. LC filing rules, rule 4, recommend following method 1; the recommended order for headings for different entities with the same initial filing elements is: forename, surname, place, corporate body, topical subject heading, title. All existing online systems examined followed method 3.

PROs AND CONs

The practice of inverting personal names is widespread in the published literature (e.g., telephone books and reference books), and therefore familiar to library users. One can argue that the logic of displaying headings for everyone with the same surname before headings for phrases beginning with the surname is even stronger than it may be for similar treatment of inverted topical headings.[3] Method 1 allows the user looking for works about a particular person with the surname "King" to pick out the correct one, unimpeded by longer phrase headings or headings for other types of entity. It also allows the user looking for works about the King family to find them outside the long list of persons named King. Users interested in a place named King can see that there is more than one place by this name and can pick out the one they are interested in. Finally, this method allows users looking for a book called *King* to find it, even if they do not know that there is a subtitle.

Once again, however, the user must know that the headings are organized in this fashion. Method 3 allows the user who knows the heading exactly (including qualifiers, subtitles, etc.) to find it without prior knowledge about the organizing principles employed (other than a knowledge of alphabetical order).

Many online systems need not design programs to arrange topical subject headings together with names and titles, since they provide a topical subject index which is completely separate from other kinds of indexes. Such systems require users to know the difference between a topical subject and a "name" or an "author"; users of such systems might be surprised to discover some of the things we classify as topical subjects, for example, performing animals (Lassie), fictitious characters (Sherlock Holmes), and proper geographic names (Rocky Mountains). Such systems may also cause confusion if users do not know in which index to look for names as subjects.

B. Name and Subject Headings for the Same Entity

EXAMPLES

King, Martin Luther, Jr., 1924–1968.	[author]
King, Martin Luther, Jr., 1924–1968.	[subject]

CURRENT PRACTICE

Both the ALA filing rules, rule 2.2, and the LC filing rules, rule 6, recommend that when both name/title headings and subject headings for the same entity are being displayed together, the name/title headings should precede the subject headings. In addition, it is recommended that various kinds of *see* and *see also* references to name/title headings should precede the name/title headings, and various kinds of *see* and *see also* references to subject headings should precede the subject headings.

PROs AND CONs

This practice is recommended by both sets of filing rules. System designers should also note the implied recommendation that a user searching for a particular entity (a person, a corporate body, a place, etc.) should be shown *both* name headings *and* subject headings, if possible, unless the user explicitly asks to be shown *only* works about the entity (i.e., subject headings). Such a process encourages serendipity on the part of the user; the user who is looking for a book of Robert Frost's poems may go home with both poems and a biography of Frost. On the con side, this practice forces the user who *is* interested only in Frost's poems to see works about Frost as well; some may feel that this practice forces users to retrieve too much.

C. Corporate Names with Subdivisions as Subjects

Should corporate names with subdivisions display after subject subdivisions of the parent body (method 1, LC filing rules), or in the same alphabet with subject subdivisions of the parent body (method 2, ALA filing rules)?

EXAMPLES

Method 1

United States. Army—Afro-American Troops.
United States. Army—Bibliography.
United States. Army—Handbooks, manuals, etc.
United States. Army—History.
United States. Army—Pictorial works.
United States. Army—Supplies and stores.
United States. Army. Air Cavalry Division, 1st.
United States. Army. Cavalry, 10th.
United States. Army. Harry Diamond Laboratories.
United States. Army. Quartermaster Corps.
United States. Army. Women's Army Corps.
United States. Army Map Service.

Method 2

United States. Army—Afro-American troops.
United States. Army. Air Cavalry Division, 1st.
United States. Army—Bibliography.
United States. Army. Cavalry, 10th.
United States. Army—Handbooks, manuals, etc.
United States. Army. Harry Diamond Laboratories.
United States. Army—History.
United States. Army Map Service.
United States. Army—Pictorial works.
United States. Army. Quartermaster Corps.
United States. Army—Supplies and stores.
United States. Army. Women's Army Corps.

CURRENT PRACTICE

ALA filing rules, rule 1, recommend following method 2. LC filing rules, 3.3.2 and 7.2, recommend following method 1. Some existing systems follow method 1 and some follow method 2.

PROs AND CONs

Method 1 allows the user interested in the Army *per se* to scan through the various topical and form subdivisions under it and notice that materials such as yearbooks are available. When these subdivisions are interfiled with the countless corporate subdivisions of the Army, they may occur hundreds of screens after the heading for the Army itself and never be noticed.

Method 2 allows the user who knows the exact form of the heading desired to find it without having to be aware of two filing orders.

D. Works of an Author as Subjects

Should the works of an author and works about the author's works be displayed before subject subdivisions under the author's name (method 1, LC and ALA filing rules), or arranged in the same alphabet with subject subdivisions under the author's name (method 2)?

EXAMPLES

Method 1

Shakespeare, William, 1564–1616.
　　Hamlet.　　　　　　　　　　　　　　　　　[the work itself]
Shakespeare, William, 1564–1616.
　　Hamlet.　　　　　　　　　　　　　[name-title added entry]
Shakespeare, William, 1564–1616. Hamlet.　　[subject heading]
Shakespeare, William, 1564–1616.　　　　　　[subject heading]
Shakespeare, William, 1564–1616
　　– Appreciation.　　　　　　　　　　　　　　[subject heading]

Method 2

Shakespeare, William, 1564–1616.
    Hamlet.   [the work itself]
Shakespeare, William, 1564–1616.   [subject heading]
Shakespeare, William, 1564–1616
    – Appreciation.   [subject heading]
Shakespeare, William, 1564–1616.
    Hamlet.   [name-title added entry]
Shakespeare, William, 1564–1616. Hamlet.   [subject heading]

CURRENT PRACTICE

ALA filing rules, rule 2.1.2, and LC filing rules, rule 7.1, both recommend that method 1 be followed. However, few existing online systems have implemented method 1, probably because of the complexity of the necessary sort programs.

PROs AND CONs

Method 1 guarantees that the user seeking a particular work will find all works related to it or about it. Method 2 scatters materials pertaining to a single work, and it may mislead a user who finds one section of entries pertaining to the work into thinking that he or she has found all pertinent items in the library. It is significant that both sets of filing rules recommend against method 2. Method 2 undermines Cutter's objects of the catalog.[4]

It is possible that better displays, with phrases supplied by the computer to guide the user, might help prevent confusion. For example, one could imagine the parts of the above display under Method 1 introduced by phrases such as, "The Author's Works," "Related Works and Works Containing This Work,"[5] "Works about This Work," and "Works about This Author."

VI. Punctuation

A. Hyphens

Should words with hyphens be arranged as if they were separate words (method 1, ALA and LC filing rules), as if each hyphenated word was a single word with the hyphen dropped (method 2), or as if each hyphenated word was a single word with the hyphen retained and given a filing value that places it ahead of alphabetic characters (method 3)?

EXAMPLES

Method 1

Post family.
Post-impressionism (Art)
Post machines.
Posters.

Method 2

Post family.
Post machines.
Posters.
Post-impressionism (Art)

Method 3

Post family.
Post machines.
Post-impressionism (Art)
Posters.

CURRENT PRACTICE

ALA filing rules, rule 1, and LC filing rules, rule 12, recommend treating a hyphenated word as if it were two separate words. Online systems can be found that practice all three methods, although the last method is found in only one online system.

PROs AND CONs

Hyphenated words present particular problems for the unwary user, who might be looking for "online," "on-line," or "on line." Users will find that systems vary in approach to the arrangement of such words and are therefore unpredictable. Let us not forget, too, that the user has no way of knowing which form will have been used in subject headings. Methods 1 and 2 appear preferable to method 3, at least, since users probably expect "on-line" to be found either as a single word or as two words, but would not expect to find it treated as a third and separate category on its own. Method 2 has the advantage that it brings together in one place "on-line" and "online" (but note that it does not bring in "on line"). However, method 2 does not function well with hyphenated headings such as "Father-son farm operating agreements," which contain a hyphenated phrase (Father-son) that no one would expect to find treated as a single word (Fatherson). Whatever method is used, cross-references should be made from other forms users might be expected to look under. Method 1 has the advantage that it is recommended by current filing rules, thus LC catalogers are likely to make the cross-references needed in systems that arrange hyphenated words as two words, i.e., cross-references from the hyphenated word as a single word. *LCSH* does in fact have the reference, "Online data processing, search On-line data processing."

B. Initialisms and Acronyms

Should an initialism or acronym that has letters separated by spaces or periods be arranged as a single word (method 1), or should each letter in the initialism or acronym be arranged as a single word (method 2, ALA and LC filing rules)?

EXAMPLES

Method 1

Bee stings.
BLAISE (Information
    retrieval system)
Bombs.
B.S.A. motorcycle.
Button industry.

Method 2

B.S.A. motorcycle.
Bee stings.
BLAISE (Information retrieval
    system)
Bombs.
Button industry.

CURRENT PRACTICE

ALA filing rules, rule 5, and LC filing rules, rules 14, 14.1, and 14.2 call for following method 2 if punctuation or spaces intervene between the letters of an initialism or acronym. Otherwise, the term is filed as a single word.

PROs AND CONs

Users have no way of knowing whether or not catalogers have represented a particular initialism or acronym with periods or spaces. Users will be even further confused by the fact that systems vary in their arrangement of initialisms and acronyms. Method 1 has the advantage that it files initialisms and acronyms the same way, regardless of the way they are represented. Users do not need to check in several different places once they learn the arrangement rule. To implement method 1, however, the computer must be programmed to recognize acronyms and initialisms and distinguish them from, e.g., forename initials of persons. Method 2 has the advantage that it is current practice at the Library of Congress, so LC catalogers are likely to make appropriate cross-references from the initialism or acronym without periods or spaces.

C. Punctuation to Indicate Subdivisions

Should the dash that signals a subdivision in printed and microform editions of *LCSH* be used in displays of subject headings in online catalogs?

EXAMPLE

Water-supply engineers— Great Britain— Biography.

vs.

Water supply engineers Great Britain Biography

CURRENT PRACTICE

Most existing systems appear to use the dash. A few, however, dispense with punctuation altogether, as in the second example.

PROs AND CONs

We hope the above example illustrates the desirability of generating the dash from the ≠x, ≠y, and ≠z subfields in the MARC format. This practice results in a much more readily comprehensible heading, and a heading that is easier to scan in a long list.

VII. Messages to the User

━━━ ▪▪ ━━━ ▪▪ ━━━

A number of works are available to give system designers guidance in designing effective and comprehensible messages for users of online public access catalogs. Everything in these works is also applicable to the design of messages for users who search using subject headings.[6] This guide attempts to discuss only some types of messages that are specific to subject searching. Ideally, messages are tailormade to fit the language of the users of the system and to fit the capabilities of the system itself. Thus it is difficult to make explicit recommendations about messages in a document such as this one. Rather, the general recommendations made by writers of the works mentioned above are made again here: that messages be brief and concise; that they use common words comprehensible to users of the catalog; and that they be courteous, tactful, and compassionate, and avoid implying ignorance or worse on the part of the novice user who is having some difficulty learning to use the system.

A. Messages Provided When No Exact Match Is Found

The following are some examples of messages given to a user of current systems when no match for a search for the term "Alligator" is found:

Ex. 1:   No records found for Alligator

Ex. 2:   No subject headings found, for reasons type h

Ex. 3:   Your subject Alligator, matches no subject

Ex. 4:   No match try related terms

Ex. 5:   Current search: bsu alligator

COMMAND->

Type HELP or press PF1 for options.

--Zero Results Screen --------------------

Alligator TERM APPEARS IN 0 SUBJECT HEADINGS

***There are no results in [SYSTEM] which match
your search request. Please verify your subject
terms in the LIBRARY OF CONGRESS SUBJECT HEADINGS
LIST (LCSH) or
the MEDICAL SUBJECT HEADINGS LIST (MeSH)
or try your search a different way. For
information on the "BROWSE SUBJECT" search, type:
HELP BSU

Ex. 6:   Browse request: B SU alligator

Browse result: 0 subject headings found

Please type HELP for information on zero

search results.

There are several problems with these messages. First,
one suspects the terminology is *not* readily comprehensible
to the average user. Do users know what "records," "subject

headings," or "related terms" are? The phrase "type h" is ambiguous. It probably means the user should press the "h" key in order to get a help message, but a user could easily interpret it to mean that somewhere in the computer is a list of reasons for not finding headings, with each reason identified by a letter of the alphabet. Secondly, several of the messages leave the user cold, with no suggestions for what to do next.

Several of the above messages repeat the term the user entered into the system. Repeating the term appears to be a good idea, as it allows the user to review the search before entering another term. The user can make sure that the next search is not a duplicate of the last. If the user has made an inadvertent typographical error (an easy thing to do), a review of the search may allow a correction on the next search.

When no exact match is found, some systems show the user the subject heading index at the place where the user-entered term would have been found if it had been in the system. This practice can be more helpful than simply telling the user there was no match when the heading used by the system (e.g., Alligators) is close to the term sought by the user (e.g., Alligator). However, when such an approach is taken, the user should be given a message to explain what has been done. For example, "We did not find your term, but here is a list of terms that are close to your term in the alphabet."[7] Failure to provide an explanation may cause the user to think that all of the displayed headings match the search; the user may be puzzled about how this could have happened!

Some systems that show the user the subject heading index, as described above, display the user's search term midway in the screen display; others place it at the top. Placing the user midway in the display (so that headings before and after the non-matching term can be seen) may more closely simulate the user's past experience with card and microform catalogs and with indexes to reference books. Whatever method is employed, the display should differentiate clearly between headings that are present in the online catalog and the user's term that is not present. Highlighting, reverse video, color, or use of asterisks or arrows might be helpful, with accompanying messages to explain them.

B. Messages Provided When a User's Search Matches a See Reference

The following are examples of messages that current online catalogs give a user whose search for "Creativity" has hit a cross-reference:

Systems in which the user must redo the search:

Ex. 1: Creativity

SEARCH: Creative ability

Ex. 2: CREATIVITY

SEARCH UNDER: Creative ability

Systems in which the user is allowed to select on the cross-reference:

Ex. 3: YOUR SEARCH: find subject Creativity

ITEMS FOUND: 0

Items with subject: Creativity were cataloged

under the term 1. Creative ability

(In this system, the user is allowed to select

line 1 and retrieve the attached records, even

though the search matched on a cross-reference.)

Ex. 4: *Line #   # Satisfiers   Term*

1   0   Creativity

2   5   Search for Creative
                                ability.

(In this system, the user is allowed to select

line 2 and retrieve the 5 attached records, even

though the search matched on a cross-reference.)

Ex. 5: *Line #   Term*

12   Creativity

(In this system, the user is allowed to choose line 12 and retrieve the 12 attached records, even though the search matched on a cross-reference. The user is not told explicitly that he has matched a cross-reference and that another term is in use.)

Ex. 6: *Line #*   *Term*

12   Creativity

Found UNDER:

Creative ability 12

(In this system, the user is allowed to choose line 12 and retrieve the 12 attached records, even though the search matched on a cross-reference.)

Ex. 7: Creativity>>Creative ability

(In this system, the user can select on the cross-reference; the search need not be redone.)

Ex. 8: Creativity

THE ABOVE VARIANT FORM HAS NO ASSOCIATED TITLES.

THE FOLLOWING RELATED TERM(S) WILL HAVE ASSOCIATED TITLES IN THE SYSTEM:

1. 12 Creative ability.

(In this system, the user can select line 1, even though the search matched a cross-reference.)

Ex. 9: Browse request: B SU CREATIVITY

Browse result: 3 subject headings found

1. Creative ability

ALSO KNOWN AS:

```
            Creativeness

            Creativity

        2. Creativity in literature.

        3. Creativity (Linguistics)

  Ex. 10: Your Subject: Creativity

        Matches: Creativity

        Known as: Creative ability

        (This system retrieved the records even though

        the user's search matched a cross-reference;

        the display informs the user that the records

        retrieved contain a different term than the one

        searched for.)
```

A number of the examples above are rather cryptic and difficult to interpret. Terms such as "cataloged under," "associated titles" and "satisfiers" are not readily comprehensible to users. The phrase "known as" implies ignorance on the part of the user— it could be read as implying, "Everyone *else* in the world calls this concept 'Creative ability.'" Such a phrase will be particularly embarrassing in cases where *LCSH* has used out-of-date terminology and is relying on cross-references from more commonly known terms to get users to the obsolete terms.

Allowing users who have searched on a cross-reference to retrieve records without reinputting the search is a user-friendly thing to do. Such systems should make clear to the user what the system is doing, however. A message should indicate that the term input by the user is not the term used by the system. The message should also clearly convey the fact that the user may choose to retrieve records attached to the term used by the system. If the system has already automatically shown the user records attached to the term, that fact should be made clear.

If a system includes the number of postings or "satisfiers" in the display, it should be made clear to the user what these numbers refer to. The cross-reference record itself should not be counted as one of the postings.

If the system does not allow the user who has matched a cross-reference to retrieve the records attached to the term used by the system, the instruction message to the user should make it clear that another search must be input. If the system-used headings are given line numbers for selection by the user, the unused heading should not be given a line number. If possible, the user should not be required to rekey the used heading, as this makes typographical errors more likely.

C. Messages to Be Provided with an Exact Match

The system should repeat the term that was entered and indicate which index the results were retrieved from if there is more than one, e.g., subject index or title index. It is helpful if the number of postings are shown to the user. However, the display of posting numbers should clearly distinguish among bibliographic record postings, authority record postings, and line numbers. Seeing all of these numbers on the screen with no labels or with cryptic labels can be quite confusing to users. An authority record should never be counted as one of the bibliographic records posted to a heading.

Ex. 1:   Current search: bsu taxicabs

COMMAND->

Type R1 (or R2, R3 ...) to retrieve the record(s)

  in a group.

Type HELP or press PF1 for options.

--Headings List Screen---------------------

TAXICABS TERM APPEARS IN 23 SUBJECT HEADINGS

23 RESULTS

  <-> NUMBER OF ONLINE RECORDS CONTAINED

    IN EACH GROUP.

R1 2 Taxicabs.

```
R2 1 Taxicabs—Argentina—Buenos Aires—History.

R3 1 Taxicabs—California.

R4 2 Taxicabs—California—Los Angeles.

R5 1 Taxicabs—Canada.

R6 1 Taxicabs—Congresses.

R7 1 Taxicabs—Design and construction.

R8 1 Taxicabs—Ecuador—Directories.

R9 1 Taxicabs—England—London.
```

Ex. 2:   Browse request: B SU CONFLICT LAWS WILLS FRANCE

Browse result: 1 subject heading found

Type D COUNTS to display the number of books
  with each heading.

Type SELECT and the heading number to search
  for books with each heading.

1. Conflict of laws—Wills—France.

D. Related Term Displays

The following are examples of displays of related terms in existing systems:

Ex. 1:   Ceylon Subject 12

ALSO LATER HEADING Sri Lanka

Ex. 2:   YOUR SEARCH: Post-impressionism (Art)

3. Post-impressionism (Art)

4. Related: Dadaism Cubism

Ex. 3:   SEARCH TERM: Ceylon

3. Ceylon

4. ALSO SEARCH UNDER: Sri Lanka

Ex. 4:   For related titles, also search for Sri Lanka

Ex. 5: Ceylon

Search also later heading: Sri Lanka

Ex. 6: R9 21 Ceylon.

= Ceylon

SEARCH ALSO LATER HEADING: Sri Lanka

Ex. 7: Ceylon

ALSO KNOWN AS:

Sri Lanka

Ex. 8: 1. 10 Ceylon

Enter "NOTE" for Notes

RELATED TERM(S) ALSO USED:

2. 2 Sri Lanka

(In this system, the user may select the
related term, if so desired. The user may also
type in the command NOTE to read the scope notes
attached to the heading and obtain a further
explanation of the relationship between the
two headings.)

Ex. 9: 9 RESULTS

D1 Post-impressionism (Art)

D2 Post-impressionism (Art)

  SEARCH ALSO Cubism

D3 Post-impressionism (Art)

  SEARCH ALSO Dadaism

D4 Post-impressionism (Art)

  SEARCH ALSO Expressionism (Art)

D5 Post-impressionism (Art)

  SEARCH ALSO Fauvism

```
D6 Post-impressionism (Art)

  SEARCH ALSO Futurism (Art)

D7 Post-impressionism (Art)

  SEARCH ALSO Impressionism (Art)

D8 Post-impressionism (Art)

  SEARCH ALSO Surrealism

D9 Post-impressionism (Art)

  SEARCH ALSO Tonalism
```

Ex. 10:Post-impressionism (Art)

```
POSSIBLE BROWSING NUMBER(S): ND1265 (SEARCH

WITH SPS/)

SEARCH ALSO UNDER:

  Cubism (28 TITLES)

  Dadaism (45 TITLES)

  Expressionism (Art) (29 TITLES)

  Fauvism (6 TITLES)

  Futurism (Art) (19 TITLES)

  Impressionism (Art) (45 TITLES)

  Surrealism (121 TITLES)

(This system suggests a classification number

search as well as related subject headings;

note the inclusion of postings with the related

subject headings.)
```

Allowing users to select related terms, rather than having to input them as searches, is helpful. If a system does not allow users to select related terms, indicating the postings for related terms may confuse users into thinking that they are allowed to select them. However, if a related term is displayed even when there are no records in the system using that term, it would be helpful to warn users of this fact everywhere the term appears.

When related terms are displayed, the fact that they are related terms should be made clear in some way, e.g., "You might also be interested in works in the following categories."

Displays are more concise and easier to scan if the related terms are displayed in one list rather than in the form of repeated "A search also B" statements, as in example 9 above.

LCSH identifies some related terms as being broader terms and some as being narrower terms. However, the terms were identified as such through a machine conversion and some of the relationships indicated may be inaccurate. Therefore, messages such as "Search also under the broader term," and "Search also under the narrower term" should probably be avoided until the subject headings can be edited more carefully.

E. Help Messages

This guide will not consider help messages in detail, since they are written to explain particular systems. We shall consider here only the messages that lead the user to the help system.

The following are examples of such messages in existing systems:

Ex. 1: Press F1 for Help

Ex. 2: F1 Help

Ex. 3: Type HELP or press PF1 for options

Ex. 4: No subject heading found, for reasons type h

It is helpful to display at all times a brief message reminding users of how to get help. Help should be obtainable at any time with a minimum number of keystrokes. A function key can be quite useful if it is clearly labeled. Clear, concise instructions are important. Not all users will know what is meant by "F1" or "PF1"; screen graphics showing pictures of keys might be useful. The ambiguity of the phrase "for reasons type h" in example 4 has already been discussed.

F. Display of Headings from Multiple Thesauri

The following are examples of displays of headings from multiple thesauri found in existing systems:

Ex. 1: B01 NEOPLASMS, NERVOUS TISSUE—//(INDX=4)

B15 NEOPLASTICISM—//(INDX=9)

(Nothing in the display indicates that the B01 heading is from *Medical Subject Headings (MeSH)* and the B15 heading is from *LCSH*.)

Ex. 2:

Hits	*Term*	*Source*
25	Clinical psychology	(LCSH)
	Clinical psychology SEE Psychology, Clinical	(Medical)
12	Psychology, Clinical	(Medical)

Ex. 3:

Term	*Source*	*Hits*
Canada—History—War of 1812	LCSH	10
Canada—History—War of 1812	CSH	50

Ex. 4:   <-> NUMBER OF ONLINE RECORDS CONTAINED IN EACH GROUP.

R1 52 Clinical psychology.

R2 94 Psychology, Clinical (MeSH)

If headings from more than one subject heading source are arranged together on the screen, clear identification of the source of each heading is necessary to explain to users why material is found under both headings. If possible, cryptic terms should be avoided. For example, in general libraries "Medical" may be preferable to "MeSH"; and in a medical school library, "General" may be preferable to "LCSH." Note, however, that the argument can be made that displaying the actual source of the terms (LCSH or MeSH) is preferable: the term "Medical" implies that all other terms are nonmedical; *LCSH* also contains medical terms, while MeSH contains general terms. If two sources of subject headings use the *same* subject heading, displays such as example 3 above can be quite confusing to users. Perhaps when the headings are the same, they should be reduced to one line in the display and the attached bibliographic records arranged in one alphabetic sequence.

Notes

1. Lois Mai Chan, "The Period Subdivision in Subject Headings," *Library Resources & Technical Services* 16 (Fall 1972): 453–459.
2. Filing "element" is defined in the LC filing rules as "one or more words that make up an integral part of a field (e.g., the surname in a personal name heading). An element and a field are identical when the field contains only one element; for example, a title." (LC filing rules, p. 9.) In a subject heading, the main heading is an element and each subdivision is an element in its own right.
3. Let us emphasize that we are suggesting that the inversion of personal names is familiar enough to users to be recognizable and predictable for them *when encountered* in a display. Systems that *require* users inputting a search to type names in inverted order are not nearly as "friendly"!
4. *Charles Ammi Cutter: Library Systematizer,* edited by Francis L. Miksa (Littleton, Colo.: Libraries Unlimited, 1977), 202–203.
5. Note that for this caption to be better designed, descriptive catalogers would need to figure out a way to code name/title and uniform title added entries to indicate why they were being made, e.g., a) for a related work, b) for a work contained within the work cataloged, etc.
6. See for example:
   Walt Crawford, *Patron Access: Issues for Online Catalogs* (Boston, Mass.: G. K. Hall, 1987); Wilbert O. Galitz, *Handbook of Screen Format Design,* 3rd ed. (Wellesley, Mass.: Q.E.D. Information Sciences, 1989); Joseph R. Matthews, *Public Access to Online Catalogs,* 2nd ed. (New York: Neal-Schuman, 1985).

7. Systems with highly structured arrangements might want to consider using the term "index," rather than the term "alphabet" here.